MONUMENTAL MILESTONES
GREAT EVENTS OF MODERN TIMES

Overview of the Korean War

A U.S. Navy Corsair fighter flies a combat air patrol (CAP) over the Inch'ŏn invasion fleet on September 15, 1950.

Mitchell Lane
PUBLISHERS

P.O. Box 196
Hockessin, Delaware 19707

Titles in the Series

MONUMENTAL MILESTONES
GREAT EVENTS OF MODERN TIMES

Overview of the Korean War

One of nineteen stainless steel statues in the Korean War Veterans Memorial in Washington, D.C.

Earle Rice Jr.

Printing   1   2   3   4   5   6   7   8   9

Library of Congress Cataloging-in-Publication Data
Rice, Earle.
  Overview of the Korean War / by Earle Rice, Jr.
      p. cm. — (Monumental milestones)
  Includes bibliographical references and index.
  ISBN 978-1-58415-695-6 (library bound)
  1. Korean War, 1950–1953—Juvenile literature. I. Title.
  DS918.R487 2009
  951.904'2—dc22
                                                                    2008020933

ABOUT THE AUTHOR: Earle Rice Jr. is a former senior design engineer and technical writer in the aerospace, electronic-defense, and nuclear industries. He has devoted full time to his writing since 1993 and is the author of more than fifty published books, including *A Brief Political and Geographic History of Latin America: Where Are Gran Colombia, La Plata, and Dutch Guiana?*, *Blitzkrieg! Hitler's Lightning War*, *The Life and Times of Erik the Red*, and *Canaletto* for Mitchell Lane Publishers. Earle is listed in *Who's Who in America* and is a member of the Society of Children's Book Writers and Illustrators; the League of World War I Aviation Historians; the Air Force Association; and the Disabled American Veterans.

PUBLISHER'S NOTE: This story is based on the author's extensive research, which he believes to be accurate. Documentation of such research is contained on page 46.

   The internet sites referenced herein were active as of the publication date. Due to the fleeting nature of some web sites, we cannot guarantee they will all be active when you are reading this book.

Contents

Overview of the Korean War

Earle Rice Jr.

*For Your Information

A British soldier of the Royal Ulster Rifles polices a crossing at the 38th parallel.

At peak strength, the forces of the United Nations in Korea numbered 932,539 on July 31, 1953. The British Commonwealth contributed more than 24,000 to this total. Their numbers consisted of armed forces from the United Kingdom, Canada, Australia, New Zealand, and a few medical personnel from India.

Clash of Arms

The world suffered about sixty-two million casualties in World War II, which ended in 1945. Less than five years later, the last thing most nations wanted was another war, but war came anyway—unwanted and *suddenly*, like a clap of thunder after an unseen flash of lightning. It came amid scattered monsoon rains and the distant rumblings of real thunder. Ironically, it came to a tiny country known as "the Land of the Morning Calm." It came to Korea on Sunday morning, June 25, 1950, when 90,000 North Korean troops crossed the 38th parallel and entered South Korea.

Korea's morning calm was shattered by a war that for decades would remain unresolved and without a formal peace agreement. U.S. President Harry S Truman could not bring himself to call it a war; instead he called it a "police action."[1] For nearly fifty years, most historians could not advance the war beyond the status of a "conflict." Today, most of the world gives it its due and calls it a war—the Korean War. This is a brief overview of how it started, how it was fought, and how it ended.

~

On August 6, 1945, the United States dropped an atomic bomb on Hiroshima, Japan. The end of World War II drew near. Two days later, the Soviet Union declared war on Japan at midnight. Supposedly, the Soviets were honoring a secret agreement between Soviet Premier Joseph Stalin and U.S. President Franklin D. Roosevelt. In February of that year, at the Crimean port of Yalta, Stalin had pledged to enter the war against Japan after the defeat of Germany. In response, Roosevelt had—among other things—conceded the return of Russian territory lost to Japan after the Russo-Japanese War of 1904–05.

After the U.S. bombing of Hiroshima, it became clear that Soviet intervention in Asia was neither needed nor wanted by the United States. A second atomic bombing, at the Japanese city of Nagasaki on August 9, assured Japan's defeat without Soviet aid. But for better or worse, an agreement is an agreement. With victory in sight, the United States could hardly deny the Soviets a share of the victor's spoils. What had seemed like such a good idea at Yalta soon turned into a troublesome political dilemma for American policy makers.

Once unleashed, Soviet armies quickly overran Japanese-held Manchuria and crossed into Korea on August 12. At about 600 miles long and averaging some 160 miles wide, the small peninsula nation was roughly the size of Southern California and was home to about thirty million people. Japan had annexed and occupied it in 1910. President Truman and his advisers feared that the Soviets might try to overrun the entire country. The United States was committed to a declaration made to Chinese Nationalist leader Chiang Kai-shek in Cairo on December 1, 1943, which stated that "in due course Korea shall become free and independent."[2] Soviet occupation of the peninsula could turn "in due course" to something closer to "never."

President Truman, to head off a dominating Soviet presence in the area, proposed a temporary division of Korea at the 38th parallel. Such a division would provide two temporary zones of military occupation to accept the surrender of Japanese troops. The Soviets were already in the northern zone and would remain there. American forces would move into the southern zone from Okinawa. The key word was "temporary." To Truman's surprise, Stalin accepted his proposal. American occupation troops began to land at Inch'ŏn during the first week in September—three weeks after the Soviet occupation.

The United States and the Soviet Union next agreed to place Korea into a five-year trusteeship. This agreement effectively "entrusted" supervisory control of the southern and northern zones of Korea to the United States and the Soviet Union, respectively. Korean patriots did not like the idea of a divided country and protested with large-scale demonstrations, but their protests went nowhere. The Americans and the Soviets moved ahead with their occupations. Their presumed goal was the independence and reunification of Korea.

The Soviets began at once to undermine the reunification process. Like the old czars of Russia, Stalin wanted to secure his border with a buffer zone of nations friendly or subservient to the Soviet Union. In the case of Korea, "friendly" meant Communist. Under Soviet supervision, a military buildup began almost at once in the northern zone. Koreans who had fought either for the Chinese or Russian Communists started pouring across the Yalu River into their homeland. By 1947, the northern sector had become an armed camp with its command center in P'yŏngyang.

The United States grew uneasy over Soviet resistance to free elections and Korean reunification. Furthermore, the threat of a Communist takeover in Korea, either by subversion or invasion, loomed large. That same year, U.S. officials referred the matter to the United Nations. The UN General Assembly resolved to hold elections throughout Korea in the spring of 1948. A nine-member UN commission went to Korea to supervise the elections. The Soviets would not allow the commission to enter its zone north of the 38th parallel.

South of the parallel, elections proceeded on schedule, and voters elected a General Assembly, which in turn chose aging patriot Syngman Rhee as its president. Rhee set up his capital in Seoul (which means "capital" in Korean). In the north, the Communists responded by forming their own government. They placed its capital in P'yŏngyang and named as its first premier Kim Il Sung, a Soviet-trained former guerrilla fighter. In just over three years after the end of World War II, two new nations emerged from a single Korea—the Republic of (South) Korea, and the Democratic People's Republic of (North) Korea. The word "temporary" had taken a giant step toward becoming permanent.

In December 1948, Soviet troops began leaving North Korea. They left behind a well-trained and equally well-equipped North Korean People's Army (NKPA). By June 1949, pressured by the Soviets and world opinion, the United States had withdrawn most of its own forces. A small force of 500 military advisers called the Korean Military Advisory Group, or KMAG (pronounced KAY-mag), remained in Korea.

On June 5, 1950, KMAG's leader, Brigadier General William L. Roberts, told a *Time* magazine correspondent: "The South Koreans have the best damn army outside the United States."[3] General Roberts was aboard ship and sailing for home on Saturday night, June 24, 1950. His time in Korea was up. The general's detractors might rightly accuse him of poor judgment, but none could fault his timing. The Korean War began at four o'clock the next morning. North Korean Premier Kim Il Sung had decided to reunite the two Koreas by force.

North Korea's assault on its southern neighbor began with a massive artillery barrage. South Korean sentries along the 38th parallel mistook the distant rumble of big guns for thunder until heavy shells came flashing and crashing among them. When the barrage lifted, ten divisions of the North Korean People's Army—about 90,000 troops—poured across the 38th parallel into South Korea. Only about one-third of South Korea's army of some 95,000 troops was deployed along the parallel. They were quickly overwhelmed by the invaders.

Some units of the unprepared Republic of Korea (ROK) army resisted bravely, but most broke and fled southward. On June 27, the UN called on member nations to send help. President Truman authorized U.S. air and naval support for the ROK. Seoul fell to the NKPA the next day. Truman then ordered U.S. ground troops into South Korea on June 30. Task Force Smith—named for its commander, Lieutenant Colonel Charles B. "Brad" Smith—arrived in Pusan, South Korea, from Japan on July 1 and began moving northward to check the NKPA advance. The North Korean invaders captured Inch'ŏn on July 3 and continued their southward sweep.

On July 5, Task Force Smith clashed with two tank-supported regiments of the NKPA's Fourth Division north of Osan. Brad Smith's unit consisted of a 406-man infantry battalion and a 134-man artillery battery from the 24th Infantry Division. The enemy elements numbered roughly 8,000 men. Action began at 8:16 A.M. and ended late in the afternoon. By then, Task Force Smith no longer existed as a military fighting unit. North Korean forces had killed, wounded, or captured about 150 Americans. The rest had scattered as far south as Taejŏn, sixty miles away.

An advancing North Korean soldier summed up the day's action in his diary that night: "We met vehicles and American POWs [prisoners of war]. We also saw some American dead. We found four of our destroyed tanks. Near Osan there was a great battle."[4] The Americans had not fared well in their first action against the North Koreans.

FOR YOUR INFORMATION

After the division of Korea in the aftermath of World War II, two powerful personalities emerged to lead the newly formed nations in the north and south of Korea. Citizens of the Republic of (South) Korea elected Syngman Rhee as their first president in August 1948. The following month, Kim Il Sung became the first premier of the People's Republic of (North) Korea. Each leader ruled with dictatorial powers, each favored reunification, and each saw himself as head of a single, independent Korea. Something had to give.

Syngman Rhee was born in Whanghae, Korea, in 1875. He learned English in a Methodist school and became an ardent Christian nationalist. In 1904, he sought higher education in the United States. He received a BA from George Washington University, an MA from

Syngman Rhee

Harvard, and a PhD in theology from Princeton University. After a brief return to Korea after the Japanese annexation in 1910, he returned to the United States in 1912 and spent the next thirty years advocating Korean independence. He became well known in Washington, D.C., and won American support in the 1948 presidential election in South Korea.

Kim Il Sung

Kim Il Sung was born as Kim Song Ju in Man'gyŏndae, Korea, in 1912. His parents fled to Manchuria in 1925 to escape Japanese rule in Korea. Kim joined the Korean guerrilla resistance movement against the Japanese occupation in the 1930s. He adopted the name of a legendary guerrilla fighter and became known thereafter as Kim Il Sung. His guerrilla activities against the Japanese caught the attention of Soviet military authorities, who sent him to the Soviet Union for military and political training. As a major in the Soviet Red Army, he led a Korean unit against the Japanese in World War II. Kim Il Sung's long relationship with the Soviets earned him their support as the first premier of North Korea.

The divided Korean peninsula now had two nations and two leaders determined to reunite the two Koreas. One wanted a democracy; the other, a Communist regime. A test of wills appeared imminent on the political horizon of both Koreas.

Soldiers of Task Force Smith arrive
station in early July 1950 on their way
the advance of North Korean invaders.

On July 5, U.S. soldiers of Task
Force Smith clashed with two
tank-supported North Korean
regiments north of Osan. A
handful of young and mostly
untested Americans tried
valiantly but unsuccessfully to
stem the tide of advancing North
Korean invaders. The roughly
8,000-man North Korean
force quickly overwhelmed the
barely more than 500 American
soldiers.

North to the Yalu

On July 7, 1950, two days after the destruction of Task Force Smith at Osan, the UN General Assembly asked the United States to serve as its executive agent in the Korean War. It also requested that the United States organize a United Nations Command (UNC) to fight the war. President Truman named General of the Army Douglas MacArthur to head the new command. MacArthur was a decorated hero of World Wars I and II who was then serving in Japan as commander in chief of the U.S. Far East Command. He immediately called for a delaying action to trade land for time until reinforcements could be rushed to the embattled peninsula.

MacArthur had already sent Major General William F. Dean's Japan-based U.S. 24th Division to stem the flow of North Koreans. By cable, MacArthur urged Washington to "grab every ship in the Pacific and pour the support into the Far East."[1] The support poured in, by both sea and air, from Japan, the United States, and points around the globe. Meanwhile, a skeleton UN force fought desperately to keep a foothold on the peninsula.

From July 8 through July 29, elements of General Dean's 24th Infantry Division fought delaying actions at Chochiwon, along the Kŭm River line, and at Taejŏn and Yechon. On July 13, Lieutenant General Walton H. Walker arrived in Taegu to take command of the Eighth U.S. Army (EUSA). A week later, General Dean was reported missing in action. His division continued its southward withdrawal toward the Naktong River without him. Forty-six days after the fall of Taejŏn, Dean's former soldiers would learn of his capture by the North Koreans.

In the meantime, in Washington, President Truman signed Public Law 624. The law extended all enlistments in the armed forces involuntarily for a period of twelve months. Coupled with an earlier draft extension and reserve call-up on June 30, help was on the way—but time was fast running out.

On July 29, General Walker told his Eighth Army, in part, "There will be no more retreating . . . There is no line behind us to which we can retreat. . . . If some of us must die, we will die fighting together."[2] His declaration became known as his "stand or die"[3] speech. The 24th Infantry Division—along with the Second and 25th Infantry Divisions, the First Cavalry Division, the First Marine Provisional Brigade, the 27th British Brigade, and eight ROK divisions—dug in along the Naktong River and prepared to stand or die. The new defense line was established on August 4. It quickly became known as the Pusan Perimeter after the port of last resort it was defending.

The Pusan Perimeter formed a rough half circle around the port of Pusan in the southeast corner of the peninsula. It stretched some one hundred miles from north to south and about fifty miles from east to west. For the next month and a half, the fate of South Korea hinged on the outcome of the fierce fighting

An aerial view of U.S. bombs destroying a railway bridge at Seoul in July 1950.

Earlier, on June 28, the South Koreans themselves blew up a heavily trafficked highway bridge at Seoul without warning, killing hundreds of fleeing South Korean soldiers and civilians.

that raged all along the perimeter. Notable battles that carved a place in the early history of the Korean War included the First and Second Battles of the Naktong Bulge, the Battle of the Bowling Alley west of Taegu, and the fight for P'ohang in the northeast corner of the perimeter.

On September 7, the First Provisional Marine Brigade withdrew from combat on the perimeter. It regrouped and boarded ship at Pusan as part of the fully assembled First Marine Division. Rumors swept across the combat zone, and most of them mentioned a place called Inch'ŏn.

Meanwhile, in Tokyo,

On June 25, North Korea crossed the 38th parallel into South Korea. Two days later, the ROK abandoned Seoul and retreated south. In September, virtually trapped at the Pusan Perimeter, U.S. and ROK forces would attempt Operation Chromite—a maneuver that would take them back to Inch'ŏn, near Seoul.

General MacArthur was working out the details of a plan to seize the initiative from the NKPA. His plan called for an amphibious landing high up on the Korean coastline near Seoul. This bold action would allow General Walker's Eighth Army to break out of the perimeter and move northward against a weakening enemy deprived of supplies. The amphibious force would then advance inland, west to east, and serve as an anvil against which Walker's army could hammer retreating enemy forces—the classic anvil/hammer military maneuver. MacArthur's plan was code-named Operation Chromite. It called for the invasion of Inch'ŏn.

Many critics opposed MacArthur's daring plan, but no one could change his mind. Fending off his skeptics, he told them, "I can almost hear the ticking of the second hand of destiny. We must act now or die."[4] In the face of further objections, he added, "Inchon will not fail. Inchon will succeed. And it will save 100,000 lives."[5] The general could not have been more right.

The invasion of Inch'ŏn commenced on September 15, 1950. It was spearheaded by the First Marine Division and backed up by the Seventh Infantry Division. Together, the two divisions made up the main elements of the Army's X (Tenth) Corps, commanded by Major General Edward M. Almond. At daybreak, a Marine battalion landed on Wolmi-do, a fortified island controlling access to Inch'ŏn harbor. Two Marine regiments carried out the main landing that evening, climbing over seawalls that formed formidable barriers. With a five-to-one advantage, they quickly overcame Inch'ŏn's 2,200 North Korean defenders. The next morning, the marines began their march toward Seoul, while the Seventh Division moved eastward to form the anvil for Walker's Eighth Army.

That same day, September 16, the Eighth Army broke out of the Pusan Perimeter and drove north. Ten days later, the Inch'ŏn and Pusan forces met

American forces landed at Inch'ŏn on September 15, 1950, during Operation Chromite.

It was the largest amphibious force assembled since World War II. General Douglas MacArthur's master strategy turned the war around in its early phases.

at Osan, the site of Task Force Smith's disastrous battle in early July. Members of the Fifth Marine Regiment raised the U.S. flag over Seoul on September 27. (It was soon replaced by the UN flag.)

On September 29, General MacArthur formally returned the South Korean capital to ROK President Syngman Rhee. In an emotional ceremony, MacArthur said, "On behalf of the United Nations Command I am happy to restore to you, Mr. President, the seat of your government, that from it you may better fulfill your constitutional responsibilities."[6] The UN commander left right after the ceremony, pipe clenched in his teeth, already planning how to finish the job.

After the UN success at Inch'ŏn and EUSA's breakout from the Pusan Perimeter, remnants of the NKPA scattered to the winds and fled toward home. MacArthur's idea of finishing the job was to destroy what was left of the NKPA, topple Kim Il Sung's regime, and reunite the two Koreas under Syngman Rhee. On October 7, the UN General Assembly issued a resolution calling for "all appropriate steps . . . to ensure conditions of stability throughout Korea."[7] It

Commander General Douglas MacArthur (center) is flanked (from left) by Vice Admiral A. D. Struble, task force commander, Major General E. K. Wright, GHQ G3 Operation and Plans; and Major General Edward M. Almond, X Corps commander.

Top U.S. commanders observe the naval bombardment of Inch'ŏn from the bridge of the USS *Mount McKinley*.

also authorized the formation of a unified government elected with UN assistance. The door to North Korea was set ajar for General MacArthur. At that moment, however, another declaration was about to take on a life of its own in the People's Republic of China (sometimes referred to during that time as Red China).

On October 8, 1950, Chairman Mao Tse-tung of the People's Republic of China issued an official order that was to profoundly influence the course of the Korean War. It began: "In order to support the Korean people's war of liberation and to resist the attacks of U.S. imperialism and its running dogs . . . I herewith order . . . the Chinese People's Volunteers to march speedily to Korea and join the Korean comrades in fighting the aggressors and winning a glorious victory."[8]

The next day, in quest of a glorious victory of his own and unaware of Mao's decision to enter the war, MacArthur launched a UN offensive into North Korea.

North of Kaesŏng, the Eighth Army's I Corps crossed over the 38th parallel and drove toward the North Korean capital of P'yŏngyang. The First Cavalry Division led the way. That same day, October 9, lead elements of X Corps's First Marine Division boarded ships at Inch'ŏn for sea movement to Wonsan on Korea's east coast. X Corps's Seventh Infantry Division embarked at Pusan on October 14, also bound for Wonsan.

On October 15, while his forces moved northward, General MacArthur flew from Tokyo to Wake Island in the middle of the Pacific Ocean for a conference with his boss, President Truman. The two leaders discussed the military situation in Korea. Truman asked, "What are the chances for Chinese or Soviet intervention?"[9] MacArthur replied, "Very little."[10]

Ten days later, Chinese Communist Forces (CCF) attacked a ROK regiment north of Unsan. The action was later identified as the CCF's first-phase offensive. On October 30, X Corps ordered the First Marine Division to replace the ROK I Corps in the Chosin Reservoir region of the eastern front.

On November 1, troops of the 24th Division advanced to within eighteen miles of Sinŭiju and the Yalu River. Near Unsan, a regiment of the First Cavalry Division came under attack by elements of the CCF 116th Division. After a flurry of stiff fighting, the attackers disappeared into the hills. Not one soldier doubted that they would be back.

FYInfo

Why China Entered the War

After World War II, Chinese Communists defeated Chinese Nationalists in a four-year civil war for control of mainland China. On October 1, 1949, Chinese Communists under Mao Tse-tung founded the People's Republic of China. When war broke out in Korea nine months later, China was neither prepared nor willing to lend support to its North Korean neighbors. Problems at home kept it too busy for more problems abroad. But when North Korea's aggression attracted direct U.S. and UN military support for South Korea, China's leaders felt forced to include Korea in their strategic planning.

In mid-1950, Mao's new regime was still struggling to occupy provinces formerly controlled by Chiang Kai-shek's Nationalists. Mao further

Chiang Kai-shek and Mao Tse-tung

planned to reclaim the Nationalist-held offshore islands, including Taiwan, to re-unify China. A Chinese takeover of Tibet also figured in his plans. After more than a decade of fighting, however, Mao's military resources were stretched thin—too thin for further involvement in Korea.

President Harry S Truman signs U.S. intervention in Korean War

A change in Mao's thinking occurred right after U.S. President Harry S Truman ordered the U.S. Seventh Fleet to "neutralize" the Taiwan Straits on June 27, 1950. His order, a warning to Mao to stay clear of Taiwan, was aimed at keeping China out of the Korean action, but it had quite the opposite effect. Mao abruptly realized that U.S. forces in South Korea could quickly pose a threat to his new Communist regime. He shifted his troops from Chinese provinces near the Taiwan Straits to northeastern provinces near the Korean peninsula.

Mao wanted to prevent a direct Chinese-American confrontation on Chinese soil. He knew that U.S. air and atomic power could devastate entire Chinese provinces. The loss of a province here and another there might bring down his entire regime, one province at a time. To counter U.S. airpower, he sought assurances of Soviet air and antiaircraft assistance in October 1950. When the Soviets refused to aid Mao, he decided to enter the Korean War. What happened next forms a part of the rest of this story.

Chinese prisoners in their standard q
and hats with ear flaps await processin

*Chinese Communist Force
(CCF) soldiers entered
Korea in mid-October 1950
and launched their first
attack on U.S. Army troops
on November 1. More than
6,600 Chinese soldiers
were taken prisoner during
the Korean War. Chinese
prisoners of war (POWs)
included almost 500 women.*

CHAPTER 3

Fallback

By mid-October of 1950, fifteen divisions of Chinese Communist Forces had slipped across the Yalu River into North Korea. Over the next several weeks, their limited attacks on advancing UN forces made it easy for General MacArthur in Tokyo to downplay the significance of a Chinese presence in Korea. He urged his field commanders to press northward with all due speed. The end of the war, as he saw it, was in sight: He would end it with one last push to the Yalu on November 24, the day after Thanksgiving.

"If this operation is successful," he told an Eighth Army corps commander, "I hope we can get the boys home by Christmas."[1] To that end, seven U.S. combat divisions and attached ROK and allied units began a two-pronged drive to the river separating China and North Korea on November 24. The 1st Cavalry and 2nd, 3rd, 24th, and 25th Infantry Divisions attacked in the west, while the 1st Marine and 7th Infantry Divisions pressed ahead in the east. Their numbers totaled about 205,000 men.

The harsh mountainous spine of the Korean peninsula separated the west and east prongs of MacArthur's offensive. Neither group could aid or communicate with the other. MacArthur's critics often point out that his strategy violated a cardinal principle of warfare—never split forces in the face of an enemy. MacArthur would pay dearly for his breach of military doctrine.

On November 25, the second day of MacArthur's offensive, the Chinese launched their second-phase offensive. Some 260,000 Chinese attackers struck with a sudden fury. They completely surprised the U.S. and UN troops and abruptly changed the course of the war. With China's intervention in Korea, MacArthur's hopeful phrase "home by Christmas" soon became a mocking reminder of MacArthur's failure to put a quick end to the war. And his failure marked the beginning of the end of his admirable military career.

In the east, Chinese forces attacked UN forces on both sides of the Chosin (Changjin) Reservoir on November 27. East of the reservoir, the CCF 80th Division struck the 3,200-man U.S. Task Force MacLean/Faith, made up of elements of the 31st and 32nd Infantry Regiments (Seventh Infantry Division). The task force bore the names of its two commanders. By December 1, the Chinese had practically annihilated it. Only 385 of its soldiers survived the slaughter. Army historian Roy E. Appleman described the carnage as "one of the worst disasters for American soldiers in the Korean war."[2]

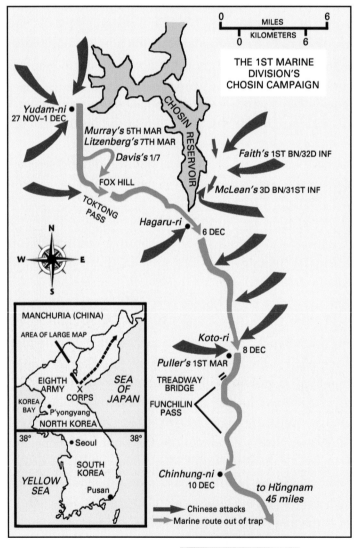

On the east side of the Chosin Reservoir, the CCF slaughtered seven eighths of the soldiers in the MacLean/Faith Task Force. On the other side, the marine (MAR) divisions fought their way south along the Road, which would take them from Yudam-ni to Hŭngnam.

West of the reservoir, three divisions of the 120,000-man CCF Ninth Army Group struck the Fifth and Seventh Regiments of the First Marine Division at Yudam-ni. The division was strung out along a narrow, seventy-eight-mile-long road. Known simply as the Road, it begins at the port of Hŭngnam and winds north through the villages of Koto-ri, Hagaru-ri (in Korean, "ri" means "village"), and Yudam-ni at the northwest end of the reservoir. Snow and ice blanketed the entire region; subzero temperatures were the norm. Then the Chinese came.

Chinese forces quickly surrounded various elements of the First Marine Division and seized control of the Road at several key points to block their retreat. Marine commander Major General Oliver P. Smith was not about to lose his division without a fight. He ordered a fighting withdrawal to Hŭngnam. The marines and allied units fought their way back to the coast through roadblocks and flank attacks with their wounded and most of their equipment and vehicles with them. They reached Hŭngnam on December 9.

The First Marine Division began its withdrawal from Hagaru-ri to Hŭngnam on December 6, 1950. The fighting withdrawal of the U.S. Marines and attached units against overwhelming Chinese forces wrote a courageous page in U.S. history.

U.S. Marines prepare to board evacuation ships at Hŭngnam harbor in December 1950.

By then, the U.S. Third Infantry Division had formed a defense perimeter around the port. The last elements of the First Marine Division and the Seventh Infantry Division passed through the perimeter on December 11 for evacuation four days later. Noted Army historian S.L.A. Marshall called their accomplishment "the greatest fighting withdrawal of modern times."[3] Few would argue with his appraisal.

Meanwhile, in the west, another major battle erupted at Kunu-ri on November 29. The village was located about twenty miles from the mouth of the Changjin River in northwestern Korea. Elements of the 130,000-man CCF 13th Army Group attacked the right flank of General Walker's Eighth Army. Chinese forces quickly surrounded, overwhelmed, and virtually destroyed the U.S. Second Infantry Division in two days of savage fighting. The division lost almost all of its heavy equipment and vehicles, along with 4,950 men reported killed or missing.

The division's history recorded the action as "a magnificent stand. . . . Even in defeat, the Indianhead [Second] Division proved to be a rock which held fast, giving other units an opportunity for survival."[4] It would take the Second Division several months to regain combat efficiency. Their stunning defeat marked the start of the longest retreat in U.S. military history.

In the face of the onrushing Chinese, MacArthur's western offensive collapsed. Units of Walker's Eighth Army pulled out of their positions and headed south in anything but an orderly withdrawal. The phrase "bug out" gave a new name to the manner of retreat of the many who abandoned weapons and equipment and fled to the south. Commanders, in many cases, lost control of their men and could not slow the rout. Americans and allied troops straggled back across the 38th parallel, singly and in small groups. Eighth Army commanders finally regained control of their units in mid-December. They quickly set up a new line of defense along the Imjin River, south of the 38th parallel and north of Seoul.

The Eighth Army suffered another blow on December 23, 1950. An unfortunate traffic accident claimed the life of its commander, Lieutenant General Walton H. Walker. He was killed when a ROK Army truck struck his jeep north of Seoul. Tough Lieutenant General Matthew B. Ridgway took his place.

On New Year's Day 1951, some 500,000 Chinese troops launched their third-phase offensive aimed at capturing Seoul again and driving UN troops farther south. They succeeded in both aims. Chinese forces recaptured Seoul on January 4, Inch'ŏn the next day, and shoved the UN forces fifty miles south of the 38th parallel to a new defense line at P'yŏngtaek-Wŏnju. UN troops checked the latest Communist offensive on January 15 and counterattacked on January 25.

General Ridgway's Eighth Army, now made up of I, IX, and X Corps, advanced to the north on either side of the Han River. I Corps held the left or west flank, X Corps the right or east flank, with IX Corps straddling the river between them. Ridgway designed his offensive to inflict maximum punishment on the enemy rather than recover lost ground. He insisted his commanders lead by example—from the front.

After observing his forces from the air, battling their way forward, Ridgway denied that they were fighting for him. Rather, he later explained, "They were fighting for themselves, with pride rekindled, and with a determination that they would never again take the sort of licking they had accepted a month before. They were back in the traditional American role of dishing out more punishment than they had to take."[5] They succeeded in shoving the Chinese north of the Han and braced for another CCF offensive. The Chinese did not disappoint them.

On the night of February 11, the Chinese launched a powerful counterattack in central Korea to initiate their phase-four offensive. They smashed through UN lines and set up roadblocks to hinder attempted UN withdrawals. X Corps fought its way back to Wŏnju, but not before the CCF had all but destroyed the ROK 8th Infantry Division. The CCF killed or captured some 7,500 ROKs and seized all of their equipment.

Beginning two nights later, 18,000 Chinese assaulted elements of the U.S. Second Infantry Division at Chipyong-ni (now Kap'yŏng), northwest of Wŏnju and east of Seoul. This time, the Indianhead Division prevailed over a much stronger enemy force. Its defense of the town marked China's first tactical defeat in the war. More important, perhaps, the victory restored the Second Division's belief in itself and symbolized its complete recovery as a fighting unit. After turning back the CCF's February offensive, the Eighth Army resumed its steady northward advance and recaptured Seoul for a second time in mid-March. By the first day of spring, it stood just below the 38th parallel.

Soldiers of the U.S. 25th Infantry Division advance in central Korea in March 1951.

After turning back the Chinese February offensive, soldiers of the U.S. Eighth Army resumed their northward march. They reached the 38th parallel on the first day of spring.

On March 21, General MacArthur received a message from the Joint Chiefs of Staff in Washington. It informed him that the president was drafting an announcement indicating the willingness of the United Nations "to discuss conditions of settlement in Korea."[6] Furthermore, strong feelings persisted within the UN "that further diplomatic efforts towards settlement should be made before any advance with forces north of the 38th parallel."[7] The Joint Chiefs asked for his recommendations.

MacArthur fired back an urgent request that "no further military restrictions be imposed upon the United Nations Command in Korea."[8] He was of no mind to accept anything less than victory in a war he had almost won. Mac-Arthur's determination to win in Korea put him at odds with President Truman—and the odds did not favor the general.

FOR YOUR INFORMATION

The U.S. Navy played a major role in the Korean War. Wars cannot be fought without men, arms, equipment, and supplies, or without some means of moving all four to the battlefield. In the case of the Korean War, some 4,914 nautical miles separated the United States from the Korean peninsula. The men, ships, and planes of the U.S. Navy delivered the troops and goods across the wide Pacific with speed, efficiency, and dependability.

During the Korean War, the Navy deployed a large number of warships to Korean waters. They included aircraft carriers, battleships, cruisers, destroyers, minesweepers, submarines, and other types of vessels. Most of these warships operated as part of Naval Forces Far East (NAVFE), commanded by Vice Admiral C. Turner Joy, and later by Vice Admiral Robert P. Briscoe. Both admirals served as chief naval adviser to General MacArthur and his successors. They also oversaw the sealift activities of the Military Sea Transportation Service (MSTS) between Korea and the United States and Japan.

The MSTS moved more than fifty-two million tons of cargo, almost twenty-two million tons of petroleum, and about five million passengers to, from, and around the Far East. Major naval operations included the Inch'ŏn invasion, the Wonsan blockade, and the Hŭngnam evacuation. Of the latter, Rear Admiral James Doyle boasted (and rightfully so), "They never laid a glove on us."[9] Other vital naval operations included knocking out enemy communications and supply lines, and providing close support of ground operations with both airpower and naval gunfire.

Of more than 5,720,000 Americans who served in the armed forces during the Korean War, some 1,842,000 served in the Navy. Seven of these sailors received their nation's highest award, the Medal of Honor. Four hundred and fifty-eight Navy personnel were killed in action and 1,576 were wounded in action.

The battleship USS *Missouri* fires a 16-inch salvo at enemy installations at Ch'ŏngjin, Korea, aimed at severing North Korean communications.

Far East commander General Matthew B̲
and Eighth U.S. Army commander Lieu
James A. Van Fleet look on as IX Co
Major General William M. Hoge stu
Ch'ŏngch'ŏn airstrip in May 1951.

Soldiers of the Eighth U.S.
Army returned to Line Kansas
on May 30, 1951. During
June 1 to 16, I and IX Corps
advanced toward Line Wyoming
in the Iron Triangle.

CHAPTER 4

The War of Movement Ends

Right after news of the president's impending announcement reached General MacArthur in Tokyo, he issued his own statement. He offered to meet with enemy field commanders to discuss means of ending the bloodshed. His offer sounded more like an ultimatum. It also put his command in the role of victor.

"The enemy . . . must by now be painfully aware that a decision of the United Nations to depart from its tolerant effort to contain the war to the area of Korea, through an expansion of our military operations to his coastal areas and interior bases," MacArthur wrote, "would doom Red China to the risk of imminent military collapse."[1] President Truman's views directly opposed those of MacArthur's. However, hoping that continued pressure would persuade the enemy to sue for peace, the president canceled his own announcement.

In the meantime, the war went on. Elements of the Eighth Army reached the 38th parallel at the end of March 1951. The question of a second UN invasion of North Korea remained unanswered. Decision time drew near.

MacArthur had made it clear that he wanted to raise the ante in Korea. He wanted to invade North Korea again. This time, however, he also wanted to blockade mainland China and attack Chinese bases and industries in Manchuria. He further wanted to use Chinese Nationalist troops from Formosa (Taiwan) against the Communists. Far from least, the general advocated using the atomic bomb to force the Chinese to quit the war if it became necessary. "There is no substitute for victory,"[2] he declared.

MacArthur's military aims flew in the face of a long-standing U.S. and UN effort to limit the fighting to the Korean peninsula. After the grim experiences of World War II, President Truman and his advisers wanted to keep that "limited war" from escalating into World War III. They also feared a possible nuclear confrontation with the Soviet Union.

President Truman finally grew tired of General MacArthur's open disagreements with national policy and challenges to his constitutional authority. He concluded that MacArthur "was unable to give his wholehearted support to the policies of the United States government and of the United Nations in matters pertaining to his official duties."[3]

On April 11, Truman relieved MacArthur of all his military duties and replaced him with General Ridgway. Ridgway in turn named Lieutenant General James A. Van Fleet as his replacement as Eighth Army commander. MacArthur returned to the United States and a hero's welcome. An initial public outcry over his dismissal faded over time.

Beginning on April 22, enemy forces launched the first step of their phase-five offensive. Twenty-one Chinese and nine North Korean divisions commenced heavy assaults in western Korea and lighter attacks in the east. Rather than expend his forces in a defensive stand, General Van Fleet ordered a step-by-step withdrawal to previously established defense positions. By the end of April, his forces had contained the enemy drive north of Seoul. When enemy forces withdrew to replenish troops and supplies, Van Fleet prepared to counterattack. But he postponed his countermove when his intelligence sources warned that he had stopped only the first step of a two-step enemy offensive.

Enemy forces renewed their attack on the night of May 15, the second step in their fifth-phase offensive. Van Fleet expected their main attack to be directed at Seoul, as before. This time, however, the enemy shifted its focus to the east-central region of the peninsula. Van Fleet quickly rushed more troops into the path of the onrushing CCF and NKPA, and brought the full force of his artillery and air support to bear on them.

General Van Fleet called for a huge artillery barrage of five times the normal output. "We must expend steel and fire, not men," he said. "I want so many artillery holes that a man can step from one to the other."[4] For five days, the air whined and the ground shook with what became known as "Van Fleet's load." By May 20, UN forces had again halted the enemy offensive after it had advanced about twenty miles, mainly as a result of massive artillery fire.

General Van Fleet immediately unleashed a counteroffensive. His Eighth Army and allied UN troops smashed their way forward to just short of Line Kansas. Line Kansas was a line of natural defenses that roughly followed the 38th parallel. It was one of several so-called phase lines used to mark the limit of advance. Line Kansas, coupled with Line Wyoming, would eventually become the cease-fire line. The general spurred his troops on, remarking, "The thirty-eighth parallel has no significance in the present tactical situation. . . . The Eighth Army will go wherever the situation dictates in hot pursuit of the enemy."[5] Van Fleet was determined to prevent the enemy from regrouping for another attack, and he succeeded. Enemy forces resisted only where UN advances threatened their supply sources. UN forces relied largely on airpower to destroy enemy supplies.

On June 1, Van Fleet launched Operation Piledriver in an attempt to secure Line Wyoming and seize control of the base of the area known as the Iron

Eighth U.S. Army commander Lieutenant General James A. Van Fleet called for a huge artillery barrage of five times the normal output. "Van Fleet's load" halted the CCF and NKPA advance.

A battery of 155-millimeter "Long Tom" rifles blast enemy positions north of Seoul in May 1951.

Triangle. This was a fairly flat area located in the mountains of east-central North Korea. It lay about thirty miles north of the 38th parallel. From west to east, the towns of Chorwon and Kumhwa (now Kimhwa) formed the base of the triangle; the town of P'yŏnggang—not to be confused with the North Korean capital of P'yŏngyang—marked its apex.

Van Fleet tapped I Corps with two divisions to hold the Eighth Army's left flank in the west. Three divisions—the First Cavalry, Third, and Twenty-fifth—were to attack the base of the Iron Triangle. On their right flank, X Corps—First Marine Division and the Seventh and Eighth ROK Divisions—advanced toward the Punchbowl, an old volcanic crater about five miles in diameter, rimmed by hills 1,000–2,000 feet high. Over the next two weeks, the Eighth Army closed on Line Wyoming "yard by weary yard, ridge by bloody ridge,"[6] as *Time* magazine reported it. Operation Piledriver succeeded in driving the enemy out of the Iron Triangle, but neither side gained control of it for the rest of the war.

By June 16, the Eighth Army occupied both Line Kansas and the Wyoming bulge. Line Kansas-Wyoming traced land highly suitable for defense. Accordingly, Washington decided to hold fast along that line and wait for a peace bid from the Chinese and North Koreans. After almost a year of fighting, the North Koreans had suffered some 600,000 casualties, including 100,000 men who had surrendered. The NKPA was all but destroyed. In only eight months, the Chinese had lost 500,000 men. It seemed more than likely that the Communists might be ready to discuss an armistice.

On June 23, 1951, Jacob Malik, the Soviet delegate to the United Nations, began the peace process. During a UN radio broadcast from New York, he said, "Discussions should be started between the belligerents for a cease-fire and an armistice."[7] When the Chinese endorsed Malik's proposal over Peiping (Beijing) radio, President Truman authorized General Ridgway in Tokyo to arrange for armistice talks with the Chinese and North Koreans. Both parties agreed to begin open talks on July 10 at the town of Kaesŏng in western Korea.

Delegates on both sides agreed for the fighting to continue until an armistice was reached. After two weeks, negotiators identified the points needed to be settled to reach a peace agreement acceptable to both sides. In succeeding weeks, the Communists began to delay. UN negotiators suspected them of

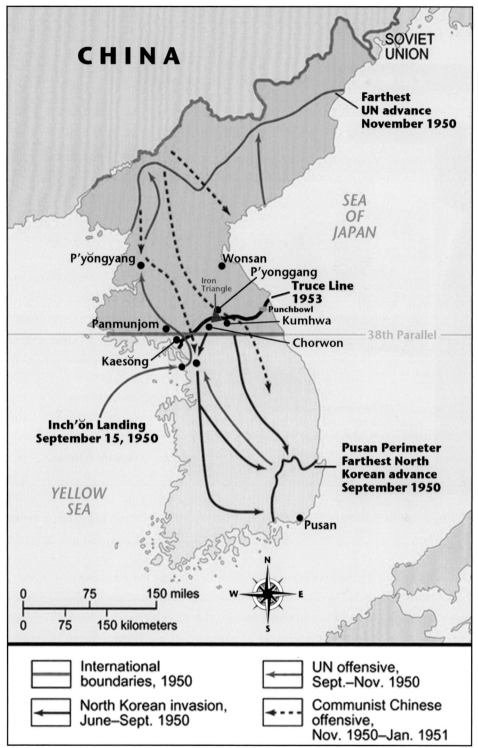

CHINA

SOVIET UNION

Farthest UN advance November 1950

SEA OF JAPAN

P'yŏngyang

Wonsan

P'yonggang

Iron Triangle

Truce Line 1953

Punchbowl

Kumhwa

Panmunjom

Chorwon

38th Parallel

Kaesŏng

Inch'ŏn Landing September 15, 1950

Pusan Perimeter Farthest North Korean advance September 1950

YELLOW SEA

Pusan

| 0 | 75 | 150 miles |
| 0 | 75 | 150 kilometers |

N
W — E
S

| International boundaries, 1950 | UN offensive, Sept.–Nov. 1950 |
| North Korean invasion, June–Sept. 1950 | Communist Chinese offensive, Nov. 1950–Jan. 1951 |

After North Korea invaded South Korea in June 1950, the NKPA advanced as far as the Pusan Perimeter in the south. UN forces mounted an offensive and drove them back, nearly reaching China. By November, the Chinese had joined the North Koreans, turning the tide once again.

Supply warehouses at the North Korean port of Wŏnsan feel the wrath of U.S. B–26 medium bombers in July 1951.

American airmen carried out an increasingly escalating air campaign against enemy troops and installations throughout the Korean War. They methodically demolished virtually everything of military significance in North Korea.

buying time to build up their military forces and thus their bargaining position. Their delays caused the talks to break down on August 22, and the war went on.

Van Fleet launched limited-objective attacks in east-central Korea. Names like Bloody Ridge and Heartbreak Ridge identified the kinds of fighting that raged across the Punchbowl area, as the Eighth Army removed enemy threats to Line Kansas-Wyoming. The Communists, perhaps influenced by the latest UN gains, returned to the conference table on October 25. This time, the talks commenced at P'anmunjŏm, a tiny village seven miles southeast of Kaesŏng.

On November 12, 1951, General Ridgway ordered UN forces to cease offensive operations and begin an active defense of Line Kansas-Wyoming. His order marked the end of the war of movement in Korea. A static war of hill battles and combat patrols took its place. Over the next twenty months, casualties would continue to mount on both sides as the peace talks dragged on.

At the outbreak of the Korean War, U.S. President Harry S Truman hoped that air and naval forces could turn back the North Korean invaders without having to commit ground forces to battle. It soon became clear, however, that airpower alone could hinder but not stop the enemy advance. Nevertheless, UN air superiority played a key role in the war.

Air operations in Korea fell into four main categories: (1) the air war over South Korea; (2) the air war over North Korea; (3) the long-range bombing campaign; and (4) the coordination of U.S. and UN air forces in all other air activities.

The air war over South Korea was conducted in support of UN and Republic of Korea ground operations. Typical missions included close air support of ground troops and the destruction or disruption of enemy lines of supply or communications. Other duties consisted of medical air evacuations and tactical airlifts of troops, equipment, and supplies, both inside and outside the combat theater.

The air war over North Korea was fought to gain and maintain air superiority over the North Korean and Chinese Communist air forces. It routinely matched U.S. F-86 Sabre jets against Russian-built MiG-15 jet fighters. F-86 pilots and others prevented Communist air action against UN ground, air, and naval forces in South Korea. American pilots achieved better than a fourteen-to-one kill ratio over their Communist opponents.

F-86 Sabre jets in Korea

In the long-range bombing campaign, U.S. B-26 light bombers and B-29 medium bombers regularly bombed military and industrial targets in North Korea. These consisted largely of bridges and hydroelectric plants along the Yalu River.

MiG-15 jet fighter

The last category consisted of the coordination of U.S. Navy and Marine Corps air operations. It also included the coordination and support of allied UN air operations. Other duties included search-and-rescue operations and the air defense of the Republic of Korea and of Japan.

Communist prisoners in this enclosure at quite peaceful, but appearances somet

Extremely overcrowded conditions at the prisoner-of-war compound at Kŏje-do hindered UN control. Lack of firm control enabled Communist leaders among the POWs to direct riots and other violent prisoner disturbances. During riots in February and March 1952, ill-trained UN guards killed 89 prisoners and wounded 166 prisoners at Kŏje-do.

Talking Peace and Making War

The United Nations Command opened the new year of 1952 on a hopeful note. On January 2, it proposed the voluntary repatriation (return) of prisoners of war who wished to return to their home countries. The Communists rejected the UNC proposal six days later. They insisted that the release and return of prisoners must not be a "trade of slaves."[1] On May 2, Communist negotiators again rejected a UNC offer for the voluntary return of POWs. As a result, both sides declared a stalemate on the POW issue.

In March, while the peace talks struggled to an impasse, the First Marine Division boarded trucks in the east and moved to the western sector of the front. One of their duties in the west was to provide a security force on an outpost overlooking P'anmunjŏm. Their mission was to sweep down on the tiny village, seize the UN negotiators, and whisk them away to safety in the event of imminent danger. While the peace talks went on at P'anmunjŏm, the marines withstood incessant mortar and artillery bombardments on an outpost dubbed "Mortar Alley."

From May 7 to 11, the UNC coped with a POW problem of a different sort—a riot at the UN POW camp on Kŏje-do, an offshore island near Pusan. Communist prisoners captured the camp commander and raised havoc for five days. They were protesting the alleged abuse of prisoners. A UN military operation finally put down the rebellion, but not before the Communists used it effectively for propaganda purposes that further poisoned the negotiating atmosphere at P'anmunjŏm.

On May 12, General Mark W. Clark, known for his leadership in Italy during World War II, replaced General Ridgway as UNC commander in chief in Tokyo. At the start of the third summer of the war, his forces were positioned along Line Jamestown, a few miles forward of Line Kansas-Wyoming.

A joint U.S. Air Force–Navy operation kicked off the summer's action on June 23 with a three-day attack on power plants along the Yalu River. U.S. planners hoped to soften the attitude of Communist negotiators at P'anmunjŏm. The attacks knocked out eleven of thirteen plants. North Korea was blacked out for two weeks, but the blackout did not alter the Communist mind-set at the peace talks. On August 29, UN air forces mounted an even larger two-night raid on P'yŏngyang. The strike left the North Korean capital smoldering, yet progress at P'anmunjŏm remained stalled.

Seasonal monsoon rains dampened the ground action during the summer of 1952, but significant hill battles broke out at various points along the line. The Chinese launched repeated attacks at Old Baldy, a hill held by the U.S. Seventh Infantry Division east of the Iron Triangle. In August, the First Marine Division fought off repeated enemy assaults on Bunker Hill, in the first major Marine ground action in the western sector. As summer moved into fall, battles at Outpost Bruce, Outpost Kelly, and White Horse Hill captured headlines in U.S. newspapers. The fall of 1952 saw further violent encounters at Triangle Hill, Pike's Peak, Sandy Hill, and Jane Russell Hill in the Iron Triangle.

On October 8, the Communists rejected the final UN offer to let teams from neutral countries deal with those POWs who declined repatriation. Under the terms of the Geneva Convention, an international agreement governing the treatment of POWs, all prisoners should be returned home once the fighting ended. In the Korean War, however, several issues complicated their return. The North Koreans had captured and drafted into their army many South Koreans. Many of those South Koreans were later captured by UN forces and did not want to return to North Korea. Similarly, many Chinese captives preferred to return to Nationalist Chinese Taiwan rather than Communist mainland China. Communist negotiators insisted that prisoners be sent back to either China or North Korea. In light of the deadlock, the UNC adjourned armistice talks "indefinitely."[2]

On October 24, Republican presidential candidate General Dwight D. ("Ike") Eisenhower all but ensured his election by promising to "concentrate on the job of ending the Korean War."[3] He further vowed "to go to Korea"[4] if elected. Eisenhower defeated Democratic candidate Adlai E. Stevenson by almost seven million votes in the November election. Meanwhile, General Van Fleet's Operation Showdown cost UN forces about 9,000 casualties against

some 19,000 Communist losses in a failed UN attempt to seize a ridgeline three miles forward of Kimhwa.

President-elect Eisenhower kept his campaign promise to visit Korea. For four days in early December, Ike donned field gear and interviewed troops and commanders in the field. After viewing the hills of Korea and talking with troops at every level, he came away convinced of the futility of continuing to expend human lives to control barren chunks of landscape. The war should be ended; the question was how. As the year 1952 drew to a close, the men of the 38th Infantry Regiment (Second Infantry Division) fought off a Chinese assault on T-Bone Hill in central Korea on Christmas Day.

On January 20, 1953, Eisenhower replaced Truman as president of the United States and commander in chief of its armed forces. How to end the Korean War became his top priority. Ike had considered using the atomic bomb, but Korea offered no real targets of value, certainly none worthy of risking World War III. He decided against the use of atomic weaponry. Publicly, however, he stressed that the stalemate in Korea was intolerable and could not be allowed to continue indefinitely. All military options, he declared, remained on the table. His public declaration, he felt, would give the Communists something to stew over.

On February 11, Lieutenant General Maxwell D. Taylor replaced General Van Fleet as EUSA commander in Korea. Van Fleet, frustrated over weak political and military decisions that had affected his command in Korea, retired from the army as a full general in April 1953. Another significant change occurred shortly after Maxwell took over in Korea. On March 5, Soviet dictator Joseph Stalin died in Moscow. With his death, a thaw in East-West relations occurred almost at once. But along Line Jamestown, the killing went on.

One of the most famous battles of the war erupted on Pork Chop Hill on March 23. It would rage on for more than three months. The outpost hill shaped like its name stood just west of the Iron Triangle. Its Seventh Infantry Division defenders clung to it desperately, courageously. Hollywood later made a film of their heroic stand starring Gregory Peck. In the end, General Maxwell ordered his soldiers to abandon the worthless piece of real estate. Its possession was not worth the life of another American soldier.

From the 26th of March through the 30th, three hills to the west of Pork Chop became emblazoned in the battle history of the U.S. Marine Corps—Reno,

Two companions help an injured UN soldier to repatriation during Operation Little Switch.

A North Korean soldier carries a wounded comrade during Operation Little Switch.

Far East commander General Mark W. Clark signs the Korean cease-fire agreement at P'anmunjŏm on July 27, 1953.

General Nam Il hands the Korean armistice agreement to North Korean Premier Kim Il Sung for signing on July 27, 1953.

Vegas, and Carson. Against all odds, the Marines lost Reno but held on to Vegas and Carson and a fourth hill named Elko. After the battle, Sergeant Roy Seabury led a detail onto Vegas to recover bodies. "[W]hat we were able to see," he wrote later, "was like something out of Dante's inferno."[5]

On March 30, Chinese Foreign Minister Chou En-lai declared that both sides should hand over prisoners not wishing to be repatriated to a neutral nation for resolution of their status. His suggestion was not unlike an earlier UNC proposal. It opened the door for a resumption of talks at P'anmunjŏm on April 26. Operation Little Switch exchanged sick and wounded prisoners during April 20–26. Peace talks finally resumed on April 26.

On June 4, the Communists at long last agreed to accept UN armistice proposals in all major respects. A final complication arose, however, when South Korean President Syngman Rhee bitterly opposed the agreement. He refused to accept truce terms that did not include the reunification of the two Koreas and allowed CCF prisoners to remain on Korean soil. After several weeks of threatening to continue the war on his own, Rhee finally relented. On July 12, in a letter to President Eisenhower, Rhee reluctantly declared that he "would not obstruct in any way the implementation of the terms of the armistice."[6]

On July 27, 1953, UN and Communist delegates signed the armistice agreement at P'anmunjŏm. At one minute after ten o'clock that evening, the guns fell silent in Korea.

Korean War Memorial
in Washington, D.C.

FYInfo

FOR YOUR INFORMATION

With the armistice agreement in place, the exchange of prisoners in Operation Big Switch began on August 5 and went on until September 6, 1953. Prisoners not wanting to return to their homelands were delivered to the Neutral Nations Repatriation Commission later in the month. A 2.5-mile-wide demilitarized zone (DMZ) was established by the armistice agreement. It straddles a military demarcation line that marks the front lines at the close of hostilities. The DMZ remains in place to this day.

South Korean military soldiers open a gate to allow a North Korean train to pass through the DMZ.

Casualty figures for the Korean War vary widely. According to mostly U.S. sources, American casualties numbered 33,651 killed in action, 103,284 wounded in action, 8,184 missing in action, and 7,140 prisoners of war. Republic of Korea military casualties totaled about 47,000 killed, 183,000 wounded, and 8,656 POWs; civilian losses approached one million dead or injured. Total UN casualties (excluding the United States) numbered 3,194 killed, 11,297 wounded, and 2,769 missing in action or captured.

The People's Republic of (North) Korea suffered casualties totaling 520,000 killed or wounded, 110,723 POWs, and civilian losses nearing one million dead or wounded. China sustained 381,374 casualties, some 360,000 killed or wounded, and 21,374 POWs. Some sources estimate that as many as four million Koreans died, and that China lost almost a million soldiers.

The Korean War devastated Korea. It ended with the boundary separating the two Koreas located pretty much where it had been at the start of hostilities. Nor did the war resolve the issue of Korean unification. Distrust between the two nations has carried over to the twenty-first century. China emerged from the war as the major military power in Asia.

From an American viewpoint, the Korean War accomplished at least three important things: It showed the world that the United States could achieve a vital national goal without resorting again to atomic force; it provided a wake-up call for the United States to rearm and stand ready to defend itself as a new superpower; and it kept South Koreans free.

The Statue of Brothers at the War Memorial of Korea in Seoul

Chapter Notes

Chapter 1   Clash of Arms

1. T. R. Fehrenbach, *This Kind of War: The Classic Korean War History* (Washington, DC: Brassey's, Inc., 1994), p. 72.

2. Stanley Sandler, ed., *The Korean War: An Encyclopedia* (New York: Routledge, 1995), p. xiii.

3. Fehrenbach, p. 8.

4. Robert Leckie, *Conflict: The History of the Korean War, 1950–53* (New York: Da Capo Press, 1996), p. 71.

Chapter 2   North to the Yalu

1. Clay Blair, *MacArthur* (Garden City, New York: Nelson Doubleday, 1977), p. 275.

2. Clay Blair, *The Forgotten War: America in Korea 1950–1953* (New York: Times Books, 1987), p. 168.

3. Ibid.

4. Joseph C. Goulden, *Korea: The Untold Story of the War* (New York: Times Books, 1982), p. 195.

5. Ibid.

6. John Toland, *In Mortal Combat: Korea, 1950–1953* (New York: William Morrow, 1991), p. 230.

7. Max Hastings, *The Korean War* (New York: Simon & Schuster, 1987), p. 121.

8. Sergei N. Goncharov, John W. Lewis, and Xue Litai, *Uncertain Partners: Stalin, Mao, and the Korean War* (Palo Alto, California: Stanford University Press, 1993), p. 184.

9. Toland, p. 241.

10. Ibid.

Chapter 3   Fallback

1. Clay Blair, *MacArthur* (Garden City, New York: Nelson Doubleday, 1977), p. 301.

2. Harry G. Summers Jr., *Korean War Almanac* (New York: Facts on File, 1990), p. 271.

3. Robert Leckie, *Conflict: The History of the Korean War, 1950–53* (New York: Da Capo Press, 1996), p. 225.

4. Max Hastings, *The Korean War* (New York: Simon & Schuster, 1987), pp. 144–45.

5. Matthew B. Ridgway, *The Korean War* (Garden City, New York: Doubleday, 1967), p. 106.

6. Douglas MacArthur, *Reminiscences* (Annapolis, Maryland: Naval Institute Press, 2001), p. 387.

7. Ibid.

8. Ibid.

9. Leckie, p. 227.

Chapter 4   The War of Movement Ends

1. Douglas MacArthur, *Reminiscences* (Annapolis, Maryland: Naval Institute Press, 2001), p. 388.

2. Ibid., p. 386.

3. Maurice Matloff, ed., *American Military History, Vol. II: 1902–1996* (Conshohocken, Pennsylvania: Combined Publishing, 1996), p. 222.

4. Robert Leckie, *Conflict: The History of the Korean War, 1950–53* (New York: Da Capo Press, 1996), p. 289.

5. Ibid., p. 290.

6. Clay Blair, *The Forgotten War: America in Korea 1950–1953* (New York: Times Books, 1987), p. 915.

7. Matloff, p. 223.

Chapter 5   Talking Peace and Making War

1. Bevin Alexander, *Korea: The First War We Lost* (New York: Hippocrene Books, 1986), p. 455.

2. Harry G. Summers Jr., *Korean War Almanac* (New York: Facts on File, 1990), p. 32.

3. James L. Stokesbury, *A Short History of the Korean War* (New York: William Morrow, 1988), p. 236.

4. Ibid.

5. Lee Ballenger, *The Final Crucible: U.S. Marines in Korea, Volume II: 1953* (Washington, DC: Brassey's, Inc., 2001), p. 172.

6. Summers, p. 49.

Chronology

1950

June 25	North Korean forces invade South Korea.
June 27	President Truman authorizes U.S. air and naval support for the ROK.
June 28	North Korean forces capture South Korean capital of Seoul.
June 30	President Truman commits U.S. ground troops to combat in Korea.
July 1	First U.S. ground troops arrive in Korea.
July 5	North Korean forces destroy Task Force Smith at Osan in first U.S. ground action of the war.
July 8	President Truman names General Douglas MacArthur to head UN Command.
August 4	Pusan Perimeter established.
September 15	First Marine Division lands at Inch'ŏn.
September 27	Seoul liberated by U.S. Marine and Army forces.
October 9	U.S. I Corps crosses 38th parallel north of Kaesŏng.
October 25	Chinese Communist Forces launch first-phase offensive against ROK Sixth Division north of Unsan.
October 26–28	First Marine Division lands at Wonsan.
November 25–27	Chinese launch second-phase offensive; attack U.S. forces along the Ch'ŏngch'ŏn River on the western front and at the Chosin Reservoir on the eastern front.
December 15	UN forces retreat to Imjin River defense line north of Seoul.

1951

January 1–15	Chinese third-phase offensive drives UN forces about fifty miles south of 38th parallel.
January 25	UN counteroffensive pushes Chinese north of the Han River.
February 11–17	Chinese launch fourth-phase offensive in central Korea.
March 27-31	Eighth U.S. Army elements reach 38th parallel.
April 11	President Truman relieves General MacArthur as Supreme Commander of UN forces and appoints General Matthew B. Ridgway to replace him.
April 22–30	Chinese launch first-step, fifth-phase offensive and are checked by UN forces north of Seoul.
May 15	Chinese resume offensive (second step, fifth phase) and advance about twenty miles.
May 21	UN counteroffensive drives Chinese north of 38th parallel.
June 1–16	UN forces advance to Iron Triangle and Punchbowl areas in eastern Korea.
July 10	UN and Chinese/NK representatives begin truce talks at Kaesŏng.
October 25	After breaking off and resuming, truce talks are moved to P'anmunjŏm.
November 12	General Ridgway orders UN forces to cease offensive operations and begin active defense of UN front approximating the 38th parallel; hill battles and static-warfare phase begin.

1952

January 1–October 8	Truce talks remain stalemated over issue of voluntary repatriation of prisoners of war; UN negotiators adjourn talks "indefinitely."
May 12	General Mark W. Clark succeeds General Ridgway as Supreme Commander of UN forces.
December 2–5	President-elect Dwight D. Eisenhower visits Korea.

1953

March 23–July 7	Pork Chop Hill abandoned to the Chinese in the war's last major hill battle.
April 20–26	Sick and wounded prisoners are exchanged in Operation Little Switch.
July 27	Korean armistice agreement signed at P'anmunjŏm.

Timeline in History

1900	Chinese peasants try to drive Europeans out of China in Boxer Rebellion.
1903	Henry Ford founds Ford Motor Company; Wilbur and Orville Wright successfully fly a powered airplane.
1908	Jack Johnson becomes first African-American world heavyweight boxing champion.
1914–18	Allied Powers—mainly Britain, France, and later the United States—defeat the Central Powers—chiefly Germany and Austria-Hungary—in World War I.
1917	Bolsheviks (Communists) seize power in Russia.
1919	Treaty of Versailles signed to formally conclude World War I.
1926	Hirohito succeeds his father, Yoshihito, as emperor of Japan.
1929	U.S. stock market collapses on October 28, "Black Friday"; U.S. securities lose $26 billion in value.
1933	National Socialists (Nazis) rise to power in Germany.
1934	Dionne quintuplets born in Callandar, Ontario, Canada; FBI agents shoot "Public Enemy Number One" John Dillinger.
1939	Germans under Adolf Hitler invade Poland; World War II begins.
1940	Ernest Hemingway publishes *For Whom the Bell Tolls*.
1941	Japanese bomb Pearl Harbor on December 7; United States enters World War II.
1945	Germany surrenders to Allies on May 8; Japan surrenders on September 2; World War II ends; United Nations (UN) Charter is signed.
1946	Winston Churchill gives "Iron Curtain" speech in Fulton, Missouri; Cold War begins.
1949	The North Atlantic Treaty Organization (NATO) is formed.
1950–53	UN forces fight North Korean and Chinese Communist Forces to a stalemate in the Korean War.
1957	Soviet Union launches *Sputnik I* and *II*, first earth satellites.
1961	Berlin Wall is constructed.
1965–75	United States and its allies engage North Vietnamese and Vietcong in the Vietnam War.
1969	U.S. astronaut Neil Armstrong becomes first man to walk on the moon.
1976	Israeli airborne commandos rescue 103 hostages held at Entebbe Airport, Uganda, by seven pro-Palestinian hijackers of Air France jetliner; thirty-one people are killed in the raid.
1979	Shah of Iran is forced into exile and is replaced by Ayatollah Khomeini.
1980	Fifty-seven people are killed in Mount St. Helens eruption in Washington State.
1987	Bill Gates, cofounder of Microsoft Corporation, becomes microcomputing's first billionaire and later the wealthiest man in the world.
1989	Berlin Wall is torn down.
1991	Cold War ends; U.S.-led coalition defeats Saddam Hussein's Iraqi forces in the Persian Gulf War.
2001	Islamic terrorists attack the World Trade Center in New York City and the Pentagon in Washington, D.C., on September 11; Operation Enduring Freedom begins in Afghanistan.
2003	U.S.-led coalition topples Saddam Hussein's Iraqi regime in Operation Iraqi Freedom (Iraq War).
2008	North Korea abandons development of nuclear weapons and is removed from U.S. list of states that sponsor terrorism.

Further Reading

For Young Adults

Feldman, Ruth Tenzer. *The Korean War.*
  Minneapolis, Minnesota: Lerner
  Publishing Group, 2004.
Rice, Earle, Jr. *Korea 1950: Pusan to Chosin.*
  New York: Chelsea House, 2003.
———. *Douglas MacArthur.* New York:
  Chelsea House, 2003.
———. *The Inchon Invasion.* San Diego:
  Lucent Books, 1996.
Santella, Andrew. *The Korean War.* Mankato,
  Minnesota: Capstone Press, 2007.
Stein, R. Conrad. *The Korean War: "The
  Forgotten War."* Berkeley Heights, New
  Jersey: Enslow Publishers, 2000.

Works Consulted

Alexander, Bevin. *Korea: The First War We
  Lost.* New York: Hippocrene Books,
  1986.
Ballenger, Lee. *The Final Crucible: U.S.
  Marines in Korea, Volume I: 1952.*
  Washington, DC: Brassey's, Inc., 2000.
———. *The Outpost War: U.S. Marines in
  Korea, Volume II: 1953.* Washington,
  DC: Brassey's, Inc., 2001.
Blair, Clay. *The Forgotten War: America in
  Korea 1950–1953.* New York: Times
  Books, 1987.
———. *MacArthur.* Garden City, New York:
  Nelson Doubleday, 1977.
Chambers, John Whiteclay II, ed. *The Oxford
  Companion to American Military
  History.* New York: Oxford University
  Press, 2000.
Deane, Hugh. *The Korean War: 1945–1953.*
  San Francisco: China Books, 1999.
Fehrenbach, T. R. *This Kind of War: The
  Classic Korean War History.* Washington,
  DC: Brassey's, Inc., 1994.
Goncharov, Sergei N., John W. Lewis, and
  Xue Litai. *Uncertain Partners: Stalin,
  Mao, and the Korean War.* Palo Alto,
  California: Stanford University Press,
  1993.
Goulden, Joseph C. *Korea: The Untold Story
  of the War.* New York: Times Books,
  1982.
Hastings, Max. *The Korean War.* New York:
  Simon & Schuster, 1987.

Leckie, Robert. *Conflict: The History of the
  Korean War, 1950–53.* New York: Da
  Capo Press, 1996.
MacArthur, Douglas. *Reminiscences.*
  Annapolis, Maryland: Naval Institute
  Press, 2001.
Marshall, S.L.A. *Pork Chop Hill.* New York:
  Berkley Publishing Group, 2000.
Matloff, Maurice, ed. *American Military
  History, Vol. II: 1902–1996.*
  Conshohocken, Pennsylvania: Combined
  Publishing, 1996.
Moskin, J. Robert. *The U.S. Marine Corps
  Story.* 3rd rev. ed. Boston: Little, Brown,
  1992.
Ridgway, Matthew B. *The Korean War.*
  Garden City, New York: Doubleday,
  1967.
Sandler, Stanley. *The Korean War: No Victors,
  No Vanquished.* Lexington, Kentucky:
  University Press of Kentucky, 1999.
———, ed. *The Korean War: An
  Encyclopedia.* New York: Routledge,
  1995.
*The Sea Services in the Korean War 1950–
  1953.* Annapolis, Maryland: Naval
  Institute Press and Sonalysts, Inc., 2000.
  CD-ROM.
Stokesbury, James L. *A Short History of the
  Korean War.* New York: William Morrow,
  1988.
Summers, Harry G., Jr. *Korean War Almanac.*
  New York: Facts on File, 1990.
Thomas, Nigel, and Peter Abbott. *The Korean
  War 1950–53.* Illustrated by Mike
  Chappell. Oxford, England: Osprey
  Publishing, 1998.
Toland, John. *In Mortal Combat: Korea,
  1950–1953.* New York: William Morrow,
  1991.
Varhola, Michael J. *Fire and Ice: The Korean
  War 1950–1953.* New York: Da Capo
  Press, 2000.

On the Internet

The Korean War: 1950–1953
  http://www.kimsoft.com/kr-war.htm
U.S. Army Center of Military History: *Korean
  War Commemorative Brochures*
  http://www. army.mil/cmh/collections/
  KW-Broch.htm

Glossary of Military Abbreviations

B-26—U.S. light bomber.
B-29—U.S. medium bomber.
bug out—To make a disorderly retreat.
CCF—Chinese Communist Forces.
DMZ—Demilitarized zone.
EUSA—Eighth United States Army.
F-86—U.S. Sabre jet fighter.
I Corps—(pronounced "Eye" Kor) U.S. First Corps.
IX Corps—U.S. Ninth Corps.
KMAG—Korean Military Advisory Group.
MiG-15—Russian-built jet fighter.
MSTS—Military Sea Transportation Service.
NAVFE—Naval Forces Far East.
NKPA—North Korean People's Army.
POW—Prisoner of war.
ROK—Republic of (South) Korea.
UN—United Nations.
UNC—United Nations Command.
X Corps—U.S. Tenth Corps.

Glossary

armistice (AR-mih-stis)—A mutual agreement to temporarily stop fighting.
defensive (dih-FEN[T]-siv)—An action or position serving to defend or protect.
demarcation (dee-mar-KAY-shun)—A boundary that delimits, sets apart, or separates.
emblazon (em-BLAY-zon)—To inscribe or adorn.
impasse (IM-pas)—A deadlock.
infantry (IN-fan-tree)—Foot soldiers.
offensive (oh-FEN-siv)—An aggressive action or campaign.
perimeter (peh-RIH-meh-ter)—The outer edge or boundary of an area or a geometric figure.
regiment (REH-jih-ment)—A military unit of ground forces organized into two or more battalions.
repatriation (ree-pay-tree-AY-shun)—The act of sending or bringing back a person to his or her own country.
subservient (sub-SUR-vee-ent)—Subordinate; acting under another's command.

47

Index